PETER DONNELLY

PHOTONS

APPELLO

First published in 2014 by Appello Press

Copyright © 2014 Peter Donnelly

All rights reserved. No part of this book may be reproduced in any form or by any electronic or mechanical means, including information storage and retrieval systems, without permission in writing from the publisher, except by a reviewer who may quote brief passages in a review.

ISBN: 978-0-9573752-2-2

Cover design and interior formatting by Kingston Gasteen (www.kingstongasteen.com)

for my father.

These are trial pieces

木漏れ日

PHOTONS

Peter Donnelly was born in Dublin in 1988. He graduated with a BA (International) and an MA in English from University College, Dublin, concentrating on *Finnegans Wake* for his master's thesis. In 2010 he began to publish poetry in journals across Ireland and within UCD, where he won the Undergraduate Poetry Award; his work has been said to create worlds in which "the familiar and the alien have been seamlessly fused together" by the 2013 *University Observer*'s Arts Editor Steven Balbirnie. This is his début collection.

Table of Contents

An Event Horizon	3
Minor Acoustics	4
Kitchen and Garden	5
Conjugations	6
Changing Guitar Strings	7
Love Poem	8
La Divina Commedia, *Inferno*, Canto X	9
Postmodern	15
Chironex Fleckeri	16
Light	17
Sound	18
The Punman's Pints at Finnegan's	19
The Persistence of Memory	20
Pixelated images projected,	21
July in Dalkey	22
Sandycove	24
The Brain	26
I: The Argument	26
II: The Cerebrum	27
III: The Cerebellum and Brainstem	28
IV: Computing	29
V: Demonium in Machina	30
Pavement Stars	32
In a darkish room dampened fluorescence	33
Vico Road	34
Crash Test Dummy	35
Spring to Summer	36
What Anxiety?	39
Who I Was	40
The Films We Watched	41
Bounce	43
Streetlights' light quicksilver-quick	44
Bling of Zero	45

The Mixer	46
Hours of Highway	48
The Sword in the Stone	49
Like Thunder	50
Circa Nine Thousand	51
Short and Sweet	53
Lucid Latency	54
Highway again:	55
Ghost of the Water	56
Nest	58
#poetry	59
Science and Violence	60
Christmas Shopping	61
Fantômes	62
July in Brussels (Boulevard du Régent)	63
Proteus Sees Light: A Suburban Scene	65
Split an Atam Like the Forty Pins in Her Hood	66
Blake's consciousness got smashed open;	67
Roadworks	68
Elegy	82

PHOTONS

An Event Horizon

The ghosts of massive stars
Are those swirling black holes
And a black hole inwardly pulls
With herculean force light from afar;
Dark matter laughs at the attempt
Of light to perform illumination
(Appreciate please my lyrical explanation);
Not even the muses' retinas are exempt,

And they saw the oddity of spacetime's rules
In the golden lightning of the sunken sun.
I consider in the interstellar dust the dying jewels
Made from fusing helium and hydrogen.
The supernova's finished and everything cools –
The light is switched off; before it was on.
And sure, light caused Wordsworth's daffodils to bloom;
Just know it had to beam through this icy vacuum,

This aggrandizing infinity of mostly emptiness
Compressed into a nutshell when man dreams.
What's up there, King of Infinite Space?
The confines outlining Psyche in this place
Are fluid as my warped definition of time,
And I have composed this rhyme
With utmost precision ad hoc,
Knowing full well the relativity of the clock.

Minor Acoustics

Hissing of cold water
On a scorching frying pan,
Coca-Cola's hushing hiss
When poured in a glass;

A wave's hushing hiss extending out on the sand.

Kitchen and Garden

The boiling has finished and the kettle
Clicks; the water begins to settle

Into a stillness, and the steam is thicker
And more defined now it is winter;

And the hibernation instinct is activated;
I am monk-like with my shivering and head

Swimming in recitation in the early morning.
The mind has finished a night of loading

Material to a place of more permanent storage.
Outside in the garden, foxes forage

At the perimeters of the cold lawn
Which since the break of dawn

Has sported its Halloween-spray white
Gloss of frost; and the bold sun is a spotlight

Pointing downwards at its moist surface
Through an aperture in the clouds.

The tea leaves imbue the water with their flavour
And my CNS is ebbing with the changing weather.

Conjugations

Reeling through verb conjugations
On a commuter train
Like a flute flying up
And down the scales:

It was sweltering on the train
Somewhere
In between
Verona and Florence

And we were attempting
To hammer
The irregularities
Of Italian grammar
In the smithy of our consciousness
For the untimely examination.

We raddled consistencies
For ourselves in the
Terrain of
Obscure tenses and moods,
Dabbing sweat from our brows
As we were swept
Into the currents of the language,

One foot on tiptoe still bobbing
On the seafloor, dancing with
And against the sea's heavy towing.

Changing Guitar Strings

I loosened them so as to remove and replace
Them and they resembled spaghetti achieving
Malleability in boiling water as they began to
Droop out of tune and tension.

My comparison is entirely apt
As music is the food of love.

Love Poem

I decided I would construe her as a dark lady,
For her eyes and hair bore the colours of autumn
Vegetation – its variations of withering brown. I saw a drum
Once and its head reminded me of her skin. In the hazy
Heat of a public place I walked the mazy
Twistings of her accented sentences and began to become
Foetal and nourished by them in each atom
Of my body; everything there was sunny and breezy.
I saw you again in the marble of the High Renaissance;
In the explosive heat of a continental July
I recall your respiration's rhythm, your eloquence
Of thought; my ejaculate on your thigh.
From these I've distilled love's absolute essence.
Your irony is shining from your dark eye.

La Divina Commedia, Inferno, **Canto X**

Part of the Sixth Circle: the Heretics. The tombs of the Epicureans. Farinata degli Uberti and Cavalcante dei Cavalcanti. The ability of the damned to see the future, and their inability to see the present.

The master walks a secret route
between punishment and a city wall,
and I'm at his shoulder, following suit.

"High virtue," I began to call,
"that demands my presence here,
speak, and satisfy my wishes in all.

"The souls that lie here – when may I peer
at them? The sepulchres are open,
but I see not one custodian near."

He: "They shall all be shut, done
and dusted when those in Jehoshaphat
recover their bodies and return.

"Epicurus and his followers, who thought
that the soul dies with the body,
here perish; see their tombs lined out.

"The information you ask of me
and your hidden desire (of which I know)
shall be granted to you finally."

I: "I did not let my speech flow
from my heart for brevity's sake –
the manner which to me you did show."

"Tuscan, you who, living, make
your way here speaking so finely,
kindly halt in your track.

"By your accent one can easily
ascertain you are of that noble land
I regret treating so harshly."

This terrifying voice sounded
from one of the sepulchres;
I moved to where my guide held ground.

He: "What are you doing? There is
Farinata who has risen,
visible from the waist upwards."

He was already locked in my vision –
the prominent forehead and chest –
all Hell held in utter derision.

Urging me on, the master pressed
against my back with his hand:
"By your words he'll be impressed."

When I had reached the tomb's end,
he gazed at me, almost with scorn.
"Who were your ancestors?": his demand.

I gave my lineage from origin,
wishing to oblige the blunt curiosity;
his eyebrow gave a tiny elevation,

and he said "That line is to my party,
to my parents, and to me, a foe;
twice I rattled your posse."

I: "You did, and they, fleeing, did go
everywhere; but they then returned.
In learning this art you are slow."

Then another figure appeared,
visible to me down to his chin;
on his knees he probably rested.

To see whether I was with anyone,
he looked all about me.
This disconfirmed, he began

tearily: "If your genius gives free
access to you in this dark jail, where
is my son? With you he'd be."

"It's not that I've come alone here –
he awaiting there ahead directs,
perhaps to who caused Guido's ire."

His words and what Hell inflicts
on him revealed his identity,
so I spoke, armed with these facts.

Straightening up, he asked with severity:
"Does my son no longer live?
Light falls not on his eyes' beauty?"

Then when I did not give
an answer at once
he lay back again in his grave.

But the one so magnanimous
for whom I'd tarried didn't even blink
or slightly alter his countenance.

Resuming, he began again to talk:
"Their tardiness in learning that art
hurts me as this tomb does my back.

"Fifty times divine light
will not shine on the ruling lady's
face before you too acquire this talent.

"But tell me, as you return to the world's
sweetness: Why is that populace so tough
against my kin in their decrees?"

I: "The damage affected was so rough
the Arbia went red with running blood;
to make us pray even it was enough."

He, sighing: "Not alone I stood,
and certainly I needed
good reason to join the brotherhood.

"You see this is where I was isolated,
where others would have had Florence
annihilated had I not interceded."

"Well, may your seed find peace,"
I said, "and please help unravel
this knot strangling my thoughts.

"If I'm correct, your temporal
predicament is that you see the past
and future, but the present is invisible."

"We see," he said, "as we are so curst,
distant things, as the farsighted do;
the Lord gives this degree of sight.

"When events are about to ensue,
we're blind; only others' words tell us
what for the living is currently true.

From this you may deduce
that our knowledge is redundant
when the door of the future shuts."

I said, with remorse for my fault,
"Tell the man who dropped down
his son has not passed on yet.

"I did not make the truth known,
but fell dumb in second guessing;
so please explain the fault is my own."

Then my teacher began calling,
so I implored the ghost
to reveal the company there dwelling.

He: "More than a thousand here rest
including the Cardinal and the second
Fredrick; I'll say no more than that."

He hid himself and I turned
to the great poet of the ancient world
while considering a pernicious word.

As we began, he asked:
"Why this unneeded vexation?"
I fully answered the question posed.

"Remember that hostile diction,"
said the sage, and pointing skywards,
"and listen now to my declaration:

"When you stand in the rays
of those eyes all-seeing and divine
you'll know your life's course."

Then to the left he began to turn,
from the wall to the zone's middle,
to a valley with a sharp decline.
Even from above the smell was vile.

Postmodern

The spaceships have landed near.
The aliens are drinking beer

With the angels, who are high as kites
On the summer-saturated lawn.
Through the sun pollen and optimism
And bits of flowers taken by eddies
Of wind turbine jocosely about

The grass and air, and my wife
Is suffering a migraine
And so becoming sibylline
With a head-splitting vision:

In the small fissures
Of her almost grammatical English
Are currents of speech
From the ethersphere, tapped into,

And I hope they'll start gushing.

Chironex Fleckeri

Instances of phantasmagoria
Ghost-like and drifting in Mediterranean waters.

This hallucination is warm and dangerous.
The light is passing through their transparent bodies,
Flitting light through and across their
Helmet-like heads,

Those venomous banshees
Gliding self-contentedly
With their punch prepared, the nematocysts
Readied for an implacable sting.

Half a million cnidocytes in each tentacle
And each tentacle sharper and more nibbed
Than a needle.

As slowly and insouciantly as
Satellites in space they move,
And we identify with their glassy, gelatinous beauty,

Their menacing majesty.

Light

Solar panels stare the sun down in California,
Absorbing the light the orb gives – the flare of Aurora.

Intermittent light, slowed down flashing
Generated by sun and cloud that afternoon.

The summer had not yet become
Conscious of itself – the heat had yet to become hot.

We were buzzing and clubbing
And the strobe lighting was
Ghoulish and beautiful.
It was a gorgeous *staccato* of photons.

Sound

A city possesses its own *forte* assonance
And it is overbearingly wonderful
For the few with the cognitive-aural
Gift.

What a wonderful chorus.
Sounds imitate other sounds
But only within the individual.
A ruptured Modern symphony
And the projection
Of internalized melody onto this
Brash *mélange* of noise.

The Punman's Pints at Finnegan's

Educande of Sorrento, they newknow knowwell their Vico's road.

"My brother Seán and I
Saw our future selves – ghosts –
In a parked car's window.

"Apparition in the reflection
And the transmigration
Giving elation: the four of us,

"*I fratelli Donnelli*, farting around there,
And then drinking Nastro Azzurro
At the Circus Maximus."

Enter the Ghost of Caesar.

The sound of Cassius's
Bottle clinking with
Brutus's in the future Killiney air.

The Persistence of Memory

I

The sea is
Deep and dense

And it leaks freely through
Your brain's crevices
And your unconscious's crevices
When you dream. This

Is when the tide rises.
Psyche surfs the moon's pull.

II

Street lights glidingly flow
Across the window panes
Of the black car on the motorway in the dark.
The machine is shiny and hard and expensive.

Waiting at a boarding gate in an airport.
His lips moving in a different time zone.

Pixelated images projected,
My dream oozes with their residue.

Tiny dancing sunspots
Zoom around my vision.

Thinned out clouds
Drift over the barbecue.

July in Dalkey

People are afraid to merge on freeways in Los Angeles.

Bret Easton Ellis

Suburbia is a desert full of
Life and its streets' people
Implode with hollow humidity when the weather

Styles itself as fierce and
Postcard-bright. July. A
Tranquilizer broadcast itself through the atmosphere

Like pollen and suburbanites
Go narrow of eye like
Snipers, descend in themselves and resemble the

Zombie pill pushers pedalling
Their bikes up the Pyrenees
On my TV. You and I waited for her Polo to

Pick us up from the path
But to me Hyde Park was
Like a river that exposed its condition in ripples

When SUVs swished and
Purred over its surface, which
Was waste and empty. My shades were eagle-eye
   golden

And occasionally the sun's
White plash would slide
Quickly across them and this to my eye was permission

To cross to the far
Side where hip hop
From her car flushed the sunlight clean of its silence.

Sandycove

I

I was willingly hemmed
Into the knitted intricacies of her prose
And let myself slither and linger
In its nooks and crannies of conception.

And my mind revelled in them
Like a mating snake,
Squeezing further iotas of the semiotic
Out in the in-betweens of the

Paragraphs' balanced flourishes
Written, I picture,
In the spectacular sun
Of the United States:

The sun is eyeballing every square picometre
Of the sliding door's large panes.

And in my own study it is bright also;
And her consciousness vibrates gently
In the light shafts and
The bookcase's rich woodwork.

The tower is all of ten minutes from here.

II

I think of it as a brick cranium
Standing its subjective ground
Against howling sea,

Holograms of green and purple light
Inside darting like fairies
Are symbols of her thought.

The three dimensions. The fourth is time,

The inside of the tower is humming
Silently in its own richness,

I am beside her sleeping summer body
And beads of sweat fly from her
Brow to her black hair
And her heart is flying with vibration
And her psyche is the atmosphere in the tower,
Shimmering, granting itself its own virtuosity.

The particles in a particle accelerator
Are the neurons in her brain.
The movement is necessarily light-quick
And in her rapid eye movement
The symbol is moving and developing.

III

The sibylline pulse in
Synaptic clefts,

ALP returns to the sea.

The Brain

I: The Argument

About fifteen hundred milligrams
Of very rich jelly
Like an organism unto itself
Inside of me.
What about the intangible self?

What I essentially am
Is this material.
Do I ebb between it
And the ethereal?
Hello there, metaphysical wit.

Aid me to straddle
The zone of this dichotomy.
You're the subject of my revision,
Which is rather an anomaly.
Consider a trillion

Individual pieces
Forming a whole.
Brain chemistry
Is essentially the human soul.
Is that not elementary?

II: The Cerebrum

I am the greatest: I am responsible
For both thought and action.
Without me what's highest in man is impossible:
Language, perception, memory, reason,
All function and coordinate in symphony
Thanks to my two hemispheres.
All mental heavy lifting is done by me:
I shed high empathy's intellectual tears;
I drive genius and genuine insight;
I'm imbued with *a priori* cognition;
I understood the nature of light,
Sound, and the solar system's motion.
I am thought's very *eidos*,
The others intellectually vacuous.

III: The Cerebellum and Brainstem

Nothing can cure the soul but the senses, just as nothing can cure the senses but the soul.

Oscar Wilde

The essence of man is not desire
Or his conscious life, which are fabrications
Of his personality, but rather his motor
Function and the body's machinations:
The rhythmic coordination of primitive man –
The speed of his feet in tune with nature
As he tears across an African plain.
Forget not, mammal, that in the rapture
Of movement and the *jouissance*
Of the sentient being (which we provide)
Is a dissipation of the repetitive voice
Which is the superego. When it has died
Into silence one returns to the womb,
To the sexual bliss of entering the tomb.

IV: Computing

Her cognition was expressed in binary code.
She was unaware of what rested in her mind's
Lower echelons. In so sophisticated a machine resides
Astonishing intricacy in any given node.
Man made the computer in his own mind's mode:
Tightly knitted interconnectivity which guides
The machine to high-powered precision, but also hides
Deleted files – deep in the recesses they're stowed.
So turn into the intangible head,
That matrix of galaxies sitting in the hardware,
Comatose now as the processor ticks over. I dread
The thought of its unconscious, that nightmare
Of beautiful darkness at the mind's seabed.
And yet her bright genius is like a sparkler at a funfair.

V: Demonium in Machina

Viruses in the software –
Demons locked in the skull,
Hidden within there.

She might be void or full
Of them, such is their subtlety.
I feel I must cull

Them from her entity;
I want her to get back to the basics
Of her virtual reality,

Clean her disk's
Memory of all impression
And of all foreign thoughts.

I will conduct this session
And she will provide her own cure,
Remove that legion

Of demons resting in her;
Let's get it back
To factory settings, *a priori*-pure.

That unconquerable black
Which shrouds what she is,
Which has suffered the attack

Of computer viruses.
But perhaps there is nothing
Inside that darkness.

I must bring
The ghosts to the surface,
Eliminate that sapping
Army of irrelevance.

Pavement Stars

Shards of broken glass
Hold bits of moonlight
In a little galaxy there
At the end of the night.

In a darkish room dampened fluorescence
In a wobbling tremble at a mirror's corner.

Dazzling dancing polka dots
After flash photography.

Vico Road

Vico Road: old arching gradients
Reclining in the sun's radiance.

Crash Test Dummy

*with the actual weight
of each hooded victim*

Seamus Heaney

*Leaning together
Headpiece filled with straw.*

T. S. Eliot

His body mass
Matched to mine,

Fine face vinyled
And emotionless

Before and after
The windscreen is smashed
To smithereens and
The hood is crushed inwards,

The cameras watching
State-of-the-art, the smoothness of the movement
Split into bits
In broken slow time
On the studied videos,

And the velocity hit backwards
In one smack by the white wall.

Spring to Summer

Burst. Then a coming forth of spring.
The scorched evenings and the parties
And uncalled-for rain at the pier. A string
Of beer cans and lights alive in the breeze
Of the now rattle by sea water, and bring
To me with a natural ineffable ease
Songs and revelations as tools to stun.
I wanted this summer joy to expire in the sun.

And yet July insists on the occasional grey day:
Warmness and cloud pressed together,
Developing of overcast on horizon and a ray
Of light stretched tight between the harbour
And the water lapping and flapping about in the bay.
He imagines the day's end: *gloire de la vie, ardeur
De la vie*. The day moves past like a movie moves
With the laughs and the jokes and the summer blues.

And the flush of green in the tree is a desert
In your heart. Dalkey holds the semblance of Italy
Or California close to its heart. Sorrento asserts
Itself against two shades of blue – sky and sea.
You told me – I'm sure you did – it'd hurt
To pass so many years on foreign shores, be
Deserts of sea away from where I was born and bred,
That I'd regret making exile my daily bread.

There's a message from home somewhere
In cyberspace resting and waiting for an opening.
On the computer screen sits a summer sun blare
Of light, dust on the screen exposed floating
As the summer spins by outside, settling there.
An overcast grows into the sky, but we go boating

Regardless, speeding into the wideness of the blue.
I hope the wideness of it wound right into you.

A V of sea foam now opens amongst waves.
We did this before, I recall, three or four years ago.
An outdoor excursion such as this saves
Us from wasting good weather. You can see the blow
Of the wind on the sea surface. The iPod plays
On a stereo. The summer hours are in their flow.
The iTunes library, the beer and the talk overlap,
But the sun's strength lets our energy sap

Into the inexorable. A ghost message on a cell
Phone, a dead battery and my head at work
Somewhere between the stern and bow. The swell
Of the sea fizzes to a hush again. There's a jerk
When strong wind expands the sail. You can tell
After a Valium-spun dream nothing will lurk
In the undertow of the vessel. A wave chops.
Our lungs won't stop when the storm stops,

Or when the hours have burned up under the sun.
Then a heatwave peaks and makes us dizzy,
Makes the sea glimmer. Whatever fun
And games take place take place beneath UV
Rays too, and the ecstasy of the sea in a run
Right through time; but one can't see
And hear simultaneously. At Dalkey Island
The cell phone rests square in my hand.

Is body wiser then than mind?
The evening creeps into being as we near
A beach party, go to the thud of Marshalls and find,
After mixing pills and strong stuff with beer
The heat in our heads conflicts with the cool of sand.

Then the next morning, waiting for a train, we're
Watching sunbeam in concentrated plash on the iron
Of the tracks. Lit cigarettes. Sleepers turn.

What Anxiety?

The best of us
Age into that density of figuration.
Old tropes swing around
And around, over and over

To the last syllable
Of recorded rhyme.
But the universe is
Still undergoing expansion.

Who I Was

That horror-movie grotesquery
And madness of the lower circles.

Higher up, I became Farinata degli Uberti,
And we verbally sparred over the Florentine turf war;
I nicked the limelight of your tour
For a certain period,

Poet.

The Films We Watched

What actually happened that night?

I remember the whiskey making
Love to my bloodstream

And the widescreen television
Bulbing its slightly eerie light

In the dark living room;
It was flickering
And flashing against the walls.

I recall pissing out in the garden also.
Oh yes, the cool

Communing with the nocturnal elms
And the particularly fatly trunked birch.
The glamorous silver of those Fellini films
And his beautiful kicking of the Catholic Church;
I've a recollection of movie stills
In my memory's hutch
From that time.
I loved my high sentence about the number nine.

My psychic database is upgrading.

Those nights were high-minded,
And Jesus we were twisted
And the theories were coming out of me
Like piss after nine cans of beer.
I said I'd die in my eighty-second year
And wondered if exile could be
Once again chic.

I opened computer windows in
My brain during that period,

And everything analogous to Shem
Came racing into me from then.
Everything electrified Ananke's spindle fibres
And pinned us to archetypes
Half-elucidated and half-invented
In my favourite novel.

Bounce

The ball traced six arches before the
Rebounding from potential to kinetic
Broke into pieces at the bottom of the
Field.

Its bounces were lub-dubs of
An accelerating heart
Or the bleeps of a life support machine
Gathering pace before lapsing to the
Single note signalling departure.

And I leathered the Nike another stretch
Down the pitch. As I ran after it,
I could see stud marks
Of pressures past.

Streetlights' light quicksilver-quick

On your phone's screen

                                          In a residential area; it

Sat glintingly and luminously
On a black car's roof that night when

I asked what time it would have been in New York.
In the distance, I heard cabs gushing away into silence

And birds had begun chirping in static trees.

Bling of Zero

Buddhists believe in Śūnyatā
Which emptiness in a shining void,
The exaltation of the number zero.
The personality beyond is nullified.
It is a prize for conquering huge fear
And the personal narrative is exposed here

To be a relativity
Taken for a truth
For virtually all of one's life –
A wasteful circular path
Which one can step outside of
When there is enough

Discipline to escape
One's own opinions,
One's own thoughts even.
Then the Heavens'
Flow arrives,
Sometimes,

And the dulled sixth
Sense is again fully activated.
As a current passes through it
The soul is charged;
And notice the voltage is running
From its centre out. The burning

Sensation in the heart
Is the purging of a repeated
False story told to oneself.
The record is not deleted,
But rather our noble aspect
Robs it of power with sudden effect.

The Mixer

An ongoing roll of hollow metal
And the shifting of grit and wet
Cement within. The cement attempts
To ascend the contour of the mixer
As it rides its gradual spins, but
Always slops and settles back to
The bottom. The movement is
River-like and constant.

Firstly they feed the cement
Into the metal mouth as a
Messy, single entity. It
Rotates, it refines. The
Steady, unglamorous groan
Of progress

Lets ring around the building site:

The clap of stone on stone, that
Irritating beep of a reversing vehicle
And the discordantly scrapey ring of
The pricking shovels all when they go vocal.
They are in awe of the indelicate mixing
Which is at the heart of the action.

Something ghostly passes within
The confines of the mixer's blackness.
It knows of no way but for around,
And around and around . . .
It is as though it has been cursed to
Some torture, some spinning diabolical
Infliction which never ends. Madness
Almost. The cement mixer is driven

By a demon indeed, but you should
See the fluid malleability, the
Infinite dexterity of the cement
When it is in its element
At the end of the process.
The form can never be
Wrenched from the matter.
The cement chugs about and
Its form chugs with it. When
Ready for spreading, it is
Rare, exalting, soul-enhancing.
The cement's soul is of the
Nature of eternity. The heavy

Stones will be figured
As the architect pleases. When
The building ascends the air,
Surrounded by the sound of
Building, it knows its mind
Resting between solid stone
Is fluid and not solid.

Cranes still hang overhead,
The sun still endures a coma
Behind lumps of cloud.
So yes, the building will be shaped
To the model of whatever
The architect desires,
But there's no turning back
When the cement has dried.
The weathering of years will
Be taken in its stride.

Hours of Highway

Batter my undersoil, my raw
Grit with tarmac so my underbody
Is covered in smoothness; the gaudy
Now disguised by highway I saw

In other counties and other countries.
My texture is unmistakable, stretching
Into a strip of forever, the pulling
Of a skin really tight under wheels.

White markings in the blur of speed
Blur into one. The whiz is one long
Single action. There is a song
Blaring into the car's air and beads

Of precipitation settle
On the window panes, shyly
Tremble, and then glide freely
Into a burst obscuring damp metal

Of the neighbouring vehicle.
A series of elongated sucks
Is born of cars and trucks,
Opening up, revving to shuttle

Into the indifferent length
Of the expanse. They fall from vision
Where sky slopes to road at horizon.
The exhaust gasps and disposes breath.

The Sword in the Stone

The strawberry grows underneath the nettle,
And wholesome berries thrive and ripen best
Neighboured by fruit of baser quality.

Metal in marble. Myth and might.
The rigid way of fate is immovable
As the prized sword itself. Men
Swarmed to the spell-possessed
Steel, tried its invincibility, and
Then left scattered when the hilt
Refused their hand.

Then her release occurred, half
By the tug of Arthur's arm
And half by his thought:
She gave and the blade escaped
The anvil. The sweetness of it
Trilled and echoed at the air.

Like Thunder

Ed elli avea del cul fatto trombetta.

My wit or my shit?
My words or my turds?
My theses or my faeces?
My vowels or my bowels?

Every writer is a shiter.

2012: my dissertation on the *Wake*,
The sort of novel to make
Even the most common chump
Meditate on his dump.

A cacophony from the wind section:
Toilets aligned in rows,
Flatulence accompanying the excretion –
Reverberation when the musician blows

A note into his mouthpiece.
Art always an expunging?
Creation itself a catharsis?
The muses when the bowels are moving?

Circa Nine Thousand

The Roman sky was bloody in colour,
The place's great characters over time
And plains of imagination
Intensify its *genius loci.*

Leurs paisible génération sont traversé les âges et sont arrivées jusqu'à nous.

The Buddhism for Europeans; gory glory.
Variations on lions and elephants,
Whole species gone into
Gratuitous butchery.

Plusieurs sont entrées dans le néant.

Figures of Vidal's Empire
Active under almost eternal archetypes;
Rome under the assault of fire;
And players
In Washington D.C.

Share their
Paradigmatic model
With those of antiquity,
Of which many are in
The *Musei Capitolini.*

Fraîches et riantes comme aux jours de bataille.

Istanbul,
Ancient beauty,
Was Constantinople and
Before that Byzantium,

Yet it sits pretty on a
Massive faultline.

Qu'autour d'elles les villes ont changé de maîtres et de noms.

Short and Sweet

The sweet creak in the crunch
Of a step in snow,
And as I traverse,
The steady flow

Of my respiration
Grounds me
After a labyrinthine
Session in virtual reality,

Which I thoroughly enjoyed.
Please dissipate my sleep;
A thought itself
Is short and sweet.

Lucid Latency

Lucid latency
In the demilitarized zone
Between sleep
And consciousness.
It is slippery there.

The stream-dream
Is a shiny hollow hologram
And a computer-generated image
In its lustre, acting out its design.

Your dream's pixelation might fizzle
Here and there in close-ups.

The whole thing, of course, is textual. And sexual
And dripping with symbol.

Highway again:
The Ballardian otherworld,
Long strips of tarmacadam
Speckled with machines.

The streams are slick
With rain and ahead of me
The sky is angled towards them.

An hour later and sections of highway
On front of me puddle in the heat

And my head is a hologram.

Ghost of the Water

I watched the image
Pulled in a bubble.

My perception was
Charged and elevated

In a tour de force of
Seeing and breathing,

Astounded by the
Soapy mix of colour.

There is always a
Parallel moment to

The moment that is
Now. What may have

Been is more alive
Than what is and

This inflicts a
Stupefying blow

Into the thought
Which nurtured a

Life washed into
Oblivion by the

Ocean of my head.

Sanctifying mist

Settles and twists

And my being is

Exalted in soullessness.

I am restored to

Fullness and the

Passing possibility

Which hitched and

Flailed at me has

Aborted itself.

Apparition gliding with
Verve and quick shimmer
Loving the pain in her
Nerve cells.

Nest

Covered by bushes
Just past the living room window
Was a wasp's nest.

Or did it belong to bees?
Anyway, I remember the sound
More than the sight, especially

After Stephen Totterdell threw a brick
Right into the exact bush
They'd colonized. "If we run quick,"

He declared, "we can escape them."
Then the sheer fear was marvellous
As the volume of the buzzing

Was cranked up high in an instant.
The steady and ritualistic air
Erupted to a new pitch of rage,

The rancorous hum
Swelling in the atmosphere
And us running to safety.

#poetry

Ceci
N'est pas
Un poème.

Science and Violence

The mushroom cloud swelled
Orgiastically in the test zone
And its huge light
Cracked the dun open:

Science and violence
Brighter than a thousand suns.

Christmas Shopping

I was jaded, I was bored,
I was with her on the highstreet.
I said to my love:
"Can I take the weight off my feet?

"Because you know we've been
Idling about here for ages.
And I know it's Christmas
But even the Magi

"Did less walking for
The newborn King.
And now that we've seen
Every diamond ring

"And glittery handbag
I'm all glamoured-out,
And I know I
Better not cry or pout

"But I have had my
Fill of Christmas shopping;
I really hope we'll
Soon be stopping

"For a pint or some shots
Of Christmas cheer
As here we've done lots –
Enough for another year."

Fantômes

Dans la nuit les fantômes passent
Comme du mercure, et restent en silhouettes
Qui glident. Au bout de la rue je m'arrête.
Une ombre lèche les murs qui frissonnent.

Les arbres sont fâchés
À cause du vent
Et les fantômes sont
Excités. Nos yeux attrapés

Dans les espaces entre leur
Mouvements fluides et beaux.
Un coup d'épée dans l'eau.
Coups de pinceau d'air.

July in Brussels (Boulevard du Régent)

after the French of Arthur Rimbaud.

for A. C.

Lined amaranth flowers on view
Along to Jupiter's plush palace.
It is you who here mixes
Your almost Sahara Desert blue.

Vine and sunned rose and fir,
Cage of the little window,
Are here enclosed in amusement! . . .
                And what
Flocks of birds! O iaio, iaio . . .

Calm mansions, old passions!
Kiosk of a lady in romantic obsession.
The arses of rose bushes.
Shadowy and low balcony of Juliet.

That Juliet: one recalls l'Henriette,
That charming train station there
In a mountain's heart, as in an orchard's profundity
Where thousands of blue devils dance in the air.

Green bench where singing to a tempestuous
Paradise is a pale Irish girl with a guitar.
In the Guyanese dining room are
Chatting children and clanging cages.

The window of the Duke's makes
Me think of snails and wood – their poison

Sleeping under the beating sun.
                            And then
It's too beautiful! We remain in silence.

Motionless boulevard without business,
No comedy or drama in this mute scene;
Infinite visions in reunion.
I know you; I admire you in silence.

Proteus Sees Light: A Suburban Scene

Evening dies into night
And the ceiling is scanned by headlights

Of vehicles passing in relative darkness.
Your light-headedness

Swelled into hallucination
As a beam's elevation

Accessed your vision,
And in your drunken condition

You observed the spectrum
Of light come

At you full-force
With protean genius,

Peaking its strength
At each individual wavelength.

Your eye knew the light's carbonation
And your creative conception

Saw synchronized swimming where it performed.
So remember how the photons fizzed.

Split an Atam Like the Forty Pins in Her Hood

Yes, I am a farsoonerite and have
Split the atom, ignoring the little pea.
Fist of the hash of Europe's lentils
For this rather wordy foodie.

Blake's consciousness got smashed open;
An angel stood still in his vision.

Roadworks

I

Action and reaction, pressure on accelerators,
The expending of energy and the corresponding
Verve of metal when the green light awakens
Movement. Cars are alerted and shocked to
Life from the hum of their daydreams:
The line of traffic lurches forward. Metal
And diesel move as slowly as opiates through
The city's veins
And I am on an expanse of tarmac and the
Streets are *slick with rain* in the blue
Of the morning.

Often the body of the road is opened:
Surgery is performed on her system
Of pipes which hiss inaudibly under
The traffic during the night and during
The day. Roadworks. Hot tarmac
Closes the hole, hardens, and then is
Grafted to the rest of the surface.

I will reopen everything and rewrite it.
You might rewrite me.

The symmetry that is always active
Deep beneath the road surface
Is silent and astounding. On one side
Of Dublin there is a leaking pipe and
The noise cannot travel along the
Density of concrete. The acoustics of
Dropping fluid are smothered by distance
And types of matter which refuse to conduct

Sound. Parts of the city are unaware of
Other parts of the city, of the smoothness
Of their workings, of the irreversible
Damage they have incurred. The
Damage has happened under the
Road and so is difficult to detect.

The city is a skin always replacing
Its cells: degeneration and death,
Renewal and life.

I love the flow
Of rubber on open road, the
Revving, the gush of air in the
Accumulation of speed. Traffic
Gathers and the momentum of
The car quickly drifts into its
Terminus.

II

An exhaust's expression
Is louder in an aged vehicle.
Its sound is corrosive to the
Peace resting in the ambience,
And it rattles the silence. Within
A body that has seen

So many straights
And turns at forty-five degrees

The internal workings rotate and age.
Its revving is electrifying
In my ear. Yet also this older vehicle which

Is nearing collapse and perhaps the
Scrapyard is readying itself for its
Release into non-being, when the
Strain on its metal and internal
Connections shall be no more.

I imagine this older vehicle's afterlife
In a scrapyard, which may indeed be
Its fate. Parts of it will
Gain a renaissance in a new car. The
Metal of the new car is created out
Of the metal of the old car and so
Really there is no new car, in the
Strict sense of the word. The new
Car is glad to have inherited the
Metal of any number of old cars
Because the old metal is moulded
To the new frame in a new way.

You'll emulsify my words into
The cement sludge of your head.

III

Heaven
And Earth may pass away but
Change will never pass away because
It is always passing away, taking
Everything in its wake with it.

IV

Rivers.

The roads resemble rivers
When the water is sullened into
Darkness by the thickening wisps
Of cloud. At traffic jams
Vehicles edge and nudge forward.
The current of the road passes through
Their ebb and flow; the light flashes
Green again, the cars go and resume
Their advance through the city's
Gullies as they fill at rush hour.

A pandemonium of multicoloured urban lighting
Is refracted and distorted by the
Film of water running down the
Windscreen. The wipers slash
In rhythmic thoughtlessness back and forth,
Sharpening the images before
The rain floods the clarity back
To a blur. Flooding and slashing,
Flooding and slashing, and

The precipitation has finished but
The already-fallen water performs
A sliding caress of the sidewalk
Before vanishing into drains:
Gravity exploits the depressions
In the road's surface and the
Fluid is swallowed by this black
Hole in the street. The rainwater
Which has been roped into the
Nothingness just below the city's
Skin by gravity will

Appear miles and miles up in the air if
                                        Given space and time

Before sliding through the atmosphere
To complete the cycle.

V

Winter in the city: the
Fallen rain tightens
Into ice in the cold of the
Night. The windows of
The cars accept the chilled
Breath of the season, the
Death in the breeze. At
Dawn we see its blanched
Mark masking the glass
Of the windscreen, its
Thorough powdering of
Lawns.

Black ice is born into
Only particular conditions:
A certain temperature after rainfall.
The silence when the car braves it
Speaks of danger. We should raise our
Gear now.

After thawing there's a
Damp hiss when
A car wheel forces water
Settled on the road into
The quick elevation of a
Spray. The droplets resettle
On the asphalt and are kicked
Skyward again with the
Passing of more rubber:

Friction and slush: action and reaction
Each day in the suburbs.

VI

The corpses of the fallen leaves
Have lost their post-mortem
Beauty on the cusp of autumn
And winter. The rainwater plasters
Them like papier mâché onto the
Grey of the pavement. See how
They suck and clutch to the stone,
And how easily and silently their
Bodies are torn when the soles
Of passing shoes are pressed to
Them.

A drier evening; walking on drier leaves:
A hushed crunch. The painful climax of
A summer day when the heat peaks, and
The sun's presence is spearing. But that
Shifting kaleidoscope of colour
Undergone by the *soleil couchant* was
Lost on me. The time when I could
See it for what it was, was not yet, that
Day in the heart of July. Mid-morning
In summer promises steady, explosive
Radiation from the sun. It gathers force
Like a wave and achieves its apex at noon,
Before submitting to the spin of gravity
At the point of the day's death. At seven,
The evening is abundant in declining warmth,
And I watch the sun slip into the traffic-light amber
Of the horizon.

Six. The cover of darkness dissolves softly
Into another day. The sun insists on pursuing
Its gradual arc across the bowl of the sky again.
The rays are staggering, the consistency of their
Presence is staggering, day after day.
This chain of blazing days
Will phase itself out in the backend of August,
And will be upset occasionally by the tumult
Of rainy weather throwing the rhythm of the
Summer.

A road glazed in heat haze
Which grows in size when
Fast cars spin more friction
Into the air with their tyres.
The shining void dissipates
From view when the
Distance between it and the
Viewer is reduced, but it is
Reincarnated further down
The tarmac; it perishes
With my approach. That's
Close enough now. Stay at
A distance and watch one
Puddle shimmer and
Skirmish with another
Like the residue of
Your drug-induced
Hallucination playing
Out on the flat of the road.

The mirage wastes to
Nothing as the sunrays
Evaporate into the
Encroaching evening

Which paints the terrain
In honeyed light
Pregnant with memory.

VII

The white spray of the plane
Scores itself into the blue of
The sky until the streak of
White falls out of thought,
Until the sky has cleaned
Itself of all traces of the
Exhalation of the plane's
Exhaust. The blue
Restores itself.

Many more moments in the
Day elapse and the strobe
Lighting of a nightclub cuts time into
Two parallel progressions
Interplaying quickly.
The pattern of the dancing
Is missing many still
Shots, is a flick book getting
Flicked. We fill in the blanks.
Holes are punched into time,
Time that is seen by the eyes
And which is based on the
Speed of light, time that is
Defined by distortion and relativity
When the speed of light is
Exceeded.

The blue of the sky in the afternoon

And the thud of the nightclub at night.

VIII

From the road I see the field
Caressed by early sunlight,
The water in cohesive
Pellets resting on the
Bends of the blades
Of grass.
My eye feeds off the
Glistening of a single pellet
Of dew. The car moves,
And the movement contrasts
With the held position of this pellet:
Motion versus stillness. As
The car passes, the moisture of
The field shifts in iridescent
Rapidity. The light reels
Through the spectral
Colours in a showing of
Newness.

The lustre lying on the leaf
After the rainfall. That shine
On sombre green. More
Moments pass and again
Drops begin their
Splattering taps on the
Leaves. The rhythm of
The dropping this time
Accelerates into the soft
Hiss of heavier rain
For several minutes,

Then wanes, then ends.

One can see
The rainbow from anywhere
On the highway.

IX

Chilled air blown in from the depth
Of winter, the sun intense and
Low on the horizon.

The face of the road adorned by cold sunburst
In December.
The sun appears pulled and bent
In the shine of passing cars. In that reflected
Light we sheath our eyesight.

The presence of the sun is so strong
Along these parallel lanes and its
Replication in a car window is exact
Until the car's passing stretches the
Angle to death and the image cannot appear.
The connection waits to occur again
Between the sun and the blankness of
Another window.

The whiteness of light
Rests on the metal of a pole which
Supports a sign saying YIELD.
The stasis of the line of traffic is
Broken, so the displacement between
Me and the pole is stripped down
More with every rotation of

The wheel. As this stripping is
Initiated, the blotch of light is
Kicked into life and like
Quicksilver it ascends the pole
And vanishes. The zipping
Upwards of the smudge of photons
On the pole could be reversed
If the traffic would reverse.
Rewind the video, I'd like to
See that one again.

X

Bad driving and then the
Flurry of
Horns. The shriek of his
Skidding wheels,
Disturbance of the rhythm
Of the road, a throwing of the unsteady
Urban beat.

The night drops and in the distance I hear
The sounds of cars from afar. Accentuated
Lapping of sea on a long strand. A sequence of images
Split into bits and sprinkled into
The melting pot of sleep. The reeling of
A slideshow of random shots. The horn
Of a car.

XI

A splendour of majesty in the brightness
Basking in sunlight

While it streams onto the
City's history-rich streets. The street I walk
Now has held its ground in spite of bombings,
Shellings, the demolishing of statues.

It has seen the ripping up of cobblestones,
Felt the hot presence of tarmac applied to
It. It has witnessed victories and defeats,
Has enjoyed and has endured.

This street knows history is but a concept,
But has felt the falling brick and the cheer
Which constitute the record.
It has felt the reality of the events which as
An ensemble are history.

Sunlight is smashed to bits
As it passes through a tree,
The leaves filtering the photons.
Fragments of the light's wholeness
Are scattered in the shadow of a car
Parked at the side of the road. The
Surrounding shade accentuates
The beauty of the brightness

Shone onto the path in
Spangled shards
By the sun.

XII

Behind
The computer is an orgy of
Overlapping wires and

Interconnections.
Cyberspace is alive in the programming
Of my dreams, vast
As the branching connections of
My neurons,
Growing, dying, mindless, enormous.

A computer slips into the semi-consciousness
Of standby mode in the lab where
I reside. Its dreams are a tapestry
Of gathered data, its processing
Suspended temporarily. It thinks
No thoughts now.
The smothered hum of its trance
In an aural blend with that of
Other electronic brains which
Mark a rectangle in the room:
The distant-lawnmower sound of
Electronic processing.

Keyboards hit in fits and stutters.
Rain falling to the window
Ledge as the wind whips
It with a sudden gale.

The strength of the central
Processing unit. It will undergo burnout
And attempt to sort and sift
Through its maelstrom of data
Hammered into the memory.
Does it understand the impossibility
Of remembering without forgetting?
Its fault is its perfection
But there has been a power
Cut, and now the awareness

Of possessed information
Has been cut short,
Temporarily removed from
That heavily wired
Skull of plastic, though
It will surf with speed
Back into consciousness again
When the life source has
Been restored.

As you think you are aware of yourself thinking.

I see a sign on the sand
That must have blown astray
From a construction site, and
The sign says

Danger

Demolition in progress

Elegy

At eighteen I had learned to hear
The heavy trochee in *under* and *solder*,
So words entered fully the sense of touch where
The strains of art go corporeal in the reader,
Where shifting brilliances brush
The physical brain and the spinal chord
With actual sensuousness – with electric flush:
He gave the world the tangible word.
The illiterate roots electrify me.
Alone I heard the word made flesh –
Echoes of onomatopoeia in his poetry
Making the thing-in-itself once again fresh
To hauling sluggish consciousness.
I'll touch base with origins and loss.